NO ROOF
BUT SKY

Poetry of the American West

NO ROOF
BUT SKY

JANE CANDIA COLEMAN

HIGH PLAINS PRESS
GLENDO, WYOMING

ISBN: 0-931271-13-4

HIGH PLAINS PRESS
539 CASSA ROAD
GLENDO, WY 82213

ACKNOWLEDGMENTS

Certain of these poems have appeared in other publications. Acknowledgment is gratefully made to:

West Branch: Neighbors, Flowering Almond,
           Folk Tales, Poor Will's Widow
Tar River Poetry: The Arrested Dance
South Dakota Review: Bird Woman, Lullaby
Snowy Egret: Blue Morning Rising
Creeping Bent: Wild Ginger
Plainswoman: Handcart Migration, Sandhill Cranes,
           A Found Poem
Embers: Pressed Flowers
Mirage: Desert Flowers, Newlyweds
Sing, Heavenly Muse: Transformations
Wanbli Ho: Wolf, Letter from San Pedro
Cottonwood: The Rainmaker
Backcountry: Potpourri
Pittsburgh Center for the Arts Magazine: Calla Lillies,
           Moonrise, Hernandez
Horizons West: Belle Starr Addresses the Sewing Circle,
           Geronimo Photographed at Fort Sill

C O N T E N T S

I. THE LONG SHADOWS

II. ORAL HISTORIES

III. THIS VALLEY, THIS SKY

PREFACE

IT WAS SUMMER in the mountains of Southeast Arizona. Day after day I sat in Archie's crumbling blue trailer listening to him spin tales while the wind raised dust-devils in the yard, and the old mule cocked an ear at the door as if he, too, were spellbound.

Archie had eyes as blue as mountain lupine. So did his sister, Edith, who also welcomed me to her house, taught me about plants and herbs, and wove a tapestry of words around us both. "Time was...," they'd say, their eyes growing distant; "I recollect that once...," and the past would be in the room with us, a living history.

What I wanted, *needed* to do, was to capture the poetry with which these storytellers spoke. It seemed wrong to record their memories, the joyousness of their speech in cryptic notes or pages of unread facts, when what we were doing was in a tradition as old as mankind—practicing the art of making the past come alive through stories.

Later I would travel the West and meet many like Archie and Edith—Indians, Hispanics, cowboys, men and women who realized the value of history and the value of words *as few, today, do.* I would live in one of Geronimo's valleys with mountains at my door and learn that earth, too, has a voice both powerful and poignant.

The essence of these mingled tongues distilled, finally, in poetry—my own and that of the people and of the places that gave us our reality and our dreams.

JANE CANDIA COLEMAN
COCHISE COUNTY, ARIZONA

I

THE LONG
SHADOWS

MESA VERDE

T HE PEOPLE OF THE stone houses are gone,
whirled like chaff over dry fields,
scattered by the war dances of dust devils.

What remains—
sculpted walls, curved shards,
small stores of corn—
says little.

What we know is that they lived like birds.
That from their doorways
they looked out and out
over shimmering trees
into the arms of sky,

and that one day, light-boned,
weightless as any winged flock
before a journey,
they rose and flew.

BIRD WOMAN
(The Bitterroot Mountains, Montana, 1805)

I KNOW this air
this deep valley
the curve of river,
trees arched like bows above.

Once I played here,
splashed, cantered, climbed,
my name a thread spun through
canyons. Sa–ca–ja–we–a...

Now I put out my hands,
cup all in them,
move faster than the bent Charbonneau,
my husband, the bearded white men
burdened with maps and curiosity.

We are all tired, hungry,
but I am flying now —
a swift at twilight,
a swallow, purple-winged,
seeking its nest.

For days I have been singing.
It is the sound of the wind,
of water carving earth,
of the lost Shoshone
weeping old names like a prayer
before the fire has burned away.

GERONIMO PHOTOGRAPHED AT FORT SILL
(1905)

YOUR FEET are clumsy, Shadowcatcher.
I heard you stumbling through the squash rows
hoping to catch me stooped,
harvesting like a woman.

Now you ask me to smile,
moon blessing the pumpkins.
You think you can steal my secrets,
my breath, my heart,

but I have no smile,
no heart, either. Not here.
The high mountains have the shape of it,
the hunting coyotes my breath.

White man, go and photograph
a howl in the night,
the shoulders of wind in the grass
and bring them back to this place.

Bring me the long shadows
of the mountains, the yellow dance
of heated valley floor.
Bring me the elusive images

of my life, and I will smile for you—
over and over—an exchange of illusions
like the dying change into light.

A FOUND POEM
(Told by a guide at Acoma Pueblo, 1983)

THIS IS THE church of Saint Esteban,
our patron.
It was built by the Spaniards
when they came
and forced their religion on us.

The twin bells in the towers
came from Mexico.
We paid for them—
two boys and two girls.

Today most young people
are going back to the old ways.
We learn the old language
from our grandfathers
who are our dictionaries.

Sometimes in the evening
when the houses are hot,
we sit on the edge of the mesa
and look out over our land.

The little children say,
'Why do you sit there?'
'What do you see?'
We tell them we are watching the sunset.

Some things cannot be spoken.

PLAINS SONG
(The Santa Fe Trail, 1840)

I'VE LEFT THE trees behind
and so must court the sky,
its distant edge a master
of disguise that shimmers,
disappears, returns
a deeper blue or radiant
with sun-struck clouds.

Chimera, I call it,
intangible as shade
or the heat of fire.
It's buffalo chips for the hearth tonight,
the crook of the moon for light.
I close no doors against the coyote's cry,
and, sleeping, have no roof but sky.

PIECE WORK
(The Oregon Trail, 1849)

MONTHS TO make a life,
a day to watch it go.
The rocking wagon stilled
and I trapped in it…
foul, hot whale belly,
a piece of sky caught
in its teeth.

From my own belly,
a cry stillborn,
eyes glued shut as if
catching sight of the world
its size defeated her.

Wash her.
Wrap her in a scrap
of quilt.
Place her in the hard
stone earth.

No mother here. No sky.
Only piece work…
hoof beats
wheels rolling over
her small, tight face.

LULLABY
(Kansas, 1874)

*"When the locusts came down, they struck the ground
so hard it sounded like hail."*

SHH! DON'T CRY. They'll steal
your breath. They're at the door
pounding like hail. And in the well
dancing on each other's backs.

Hush now! Screaming won't help.
I tried that, too, when they chewed
my hair and ate my skirt,
the grass-green one I loved.

No one heard.

Sleep! In the morning the sky
will be blue again. I promise.
I'll make it so.
Everything changes.
Even what we believe.
Even faith
    even hope
       even love…

THE HANDCART MIGRATION

YOU ARE SIXTEEN. Young enough
    to be lured by adventure,
    to believe in freedom
    even as a Mormon wife.
You never dreamed the dancing prairie
could be a prison and you shackled
to a wheelbarrow pushing West.
There's no road but the path
of the sun, the bent grass behind you.
No sound but the wind in your ears
and your own footsteps,
slower now, their lightness lost.

What you dream of is water,
the curling of waves, the shock
of a stream licking flesh.
Your sweat dries quick as it comes,
and even your tears have gone.
You'd splash down in a puddle
if you found one,
sing like a migrating bird,
your voice harsh from drought.
You sing now to cheer your sisters
trundling beside you like unkempt hay wagons.
Then you're silent. The wind steals
your music for its own,
and spit's too scarce to whistle.

You bend your shoulders to the push,
move your legs to the heart's rhythm.
You think you'll never be soft
again, or dance, light as air,
no shadows in you.

_____

*In 1856, several parties of Mormons walked, pushing wheelbarrows, from
Iowa City to Salt Lake. Many of those were young women.*

19

BELLE STARR ADDRESSES THE SEWING CIRCLE
(Indian Territory, 1883)

DAMN PROPRIETY! I've got life in me
and love, too. I wasn't made for parlors,
teas, fancy talk with ladies.
Give me a man any time. Give me a horse,
a good bay with heart and bottom
and nothing in front of us.

You want to know the truth?
The land's in me, too; the time it takes
to get from mountains to the river; the figuring how.
And the colors. No fancy-house pinks and whites;
earth's colors and how the sky fires up to meet them
like bodies come together.

Yeah, I wear my plumes, my velvet skirts, a petticoat
to hide my legs, but I know what they're for.
Walking. Wrapping round a horse. A man
whenever one comes who's big enough to know
I can't be tied, stepped on, used for planting
like the ground and left.

You want to know what a woman's for?
Course not. Better condemn me without hearing.
But I'll tell you anyhow.
A woman's for going on with.
For laughter.
For holding when a man can't hold no more,
maybe don't want to.
For slaking thirst like water from a deep well.

Jest like a man, a woman's got courage
and dreams in her. And hunger, too,
that can't be bought. Jest like a man
I set my sights as far as I can see
and ride for it, proud of my dust.

What's that? Die a proper death? Forgiveness?
For what, ma'am? And what's proper?
Hell, you go on stitching them roses,
them pretty words you hang on the wall.
Keep your knees tight together like your mouth
and I'll go find forgiveness, all I want,
by holding out my arms. We'll see who dies happiest
or best. Regrets kill quicker than disease, ma'am,
and boredom's next. You remember that.
I ain't got time.

GOLD DUST
(The Mormon Trail)

I CLOSED THE doors and left them...
bureaus, chairs, a good iron stove.
But roses? Scarlet bergamot?
The blue spikes of rosemary?
Leave those quick and lovely children?

So I brought them...seeds, slips, roots
wrapped against weather, nurtured
in my apron pocket.
No one will say I must abandon them
to lighten the load.
I will disappoint thieves,
impress Indians with holy madness
for I touch them like a rosary,
repeat their names and know with each
a day, a moment gladly spent.

And each day's march has precedent
for Mormons brought the seeds
of sunflowers to mark their way,
stout wives in wagons flinging gold behind,
and now the whole trail's yellow,
firmly rooted in fragility.

MAIL ORDER BRIDE
(Dakota Territory, 1884)

IT'S NOT I HAVEN'T been asked, mind you.
I could've stayed home and done as well,
but I had a yen for travel.
"Go West, young lady," I says to myself.
So here I am, and I must say,
it's not what I expected.

Why, there's not even a sidewalk,
just boards and mud enough to drown in.
I hope you'll remember to scrape your boots, sir
before you come in my parlor.
No parlor? What, then? One room's all?
Dear me. I was raised for better things,
but well, I'm here now. I'll make do.
Curtains'll help some, a bit of paper on the walls,
a rug or two. I braided one while on the way.
Idle hands are sinful ones, I say.

Now, sir! I've only just arrived and haste's
indecent...kind of. I like to do things proper.
You'll trim your beard come morning,
my skin's not used to it, nor to this weather.
No sheets for the bed! No coverlet!
No bed at all but this rough place!

Oh my, I'm glad I've come. You need
a woman's hands around you, anyone can see.
Best bolt the door.
We'll have our heads on straighter
come the morning.

EARLY PHOTOGRAPH: NEBRASKA FAMILY WITH ORGAN
(1888)

HERE'S A PICTURE for the folks back home:
corrals with fat cattle, mules, a horse or two,
and back of them the planted fields.
In the center, near the cottonwood
beside the spring, Montgomery Ward's best
Windsor organ; carved, rubbed, polished, plush,
"Perfect in every respect."

Next to it, Fern and Maybelle, Ida Jean and me,
and Billy on the stool. Then Jesse smiling
on the other side and Hank and Early off
a little ways. A proper family
in a proper place, with music, too.
We can all play a mite.
The instruction book came free.

No need to photograph the soddy,
sunflowers on the roof,
grass whiskers round the door.
Who'd understand that in Pennsylvania?
They'd see the dirt house and say,
"What a hard life our Anna has,"
without knowing the pleasures.
How the yellow grass sings to itself
come evening; how the cottonwood dances,
and the larks fly sky high.

A SOILED DOVE
(Dodge City, Tombstone, Missoula, Anywhere...)

THOSE FIRST TIMES you shut your eyes.
You don't want to know whose face
it is or what his hands intend,
or watch him leave you, nameless, in the dark.

At least your belly's full, and there's a roof.
You buy whiskey now and then, a ribbon, lace.
Living's better than dying
isn't it? Anything's better

than starvation, the old cold
fingering you worse than any man,
your own breath stinking,
coming quick and shallow.

Here you've got voices, lights,
gunshots and music, the sounds
of love and laughter. You could scream
remembering the prairie silence,

no one on it but yourself and dread,
nights so thick they choked you.
You beat your hands raw
on the dark faces of mountains.

Now you hold tight to whoever comes,
wrap yourself around him
and pray to Jesus after...
for better luck next time round.

FLOWER PATCH : A QUILT
(The Staked Plains, 1900)

YOU GOT TO make quilts thick,
the wind comes through so bad.
You use good, smooth cotton,
take care with your stitches,
match your colors careful
and hope you don't run out of scraps.

Outside it's brown, dull yellow,
flat like a table. You can see the weather
coming—tornadoes, rain, the yellow dust.
You watch the clouds awhile,
that's all there is to see.
Then you get back to work
making a Flower Patch just for relief.

DESERT FLOWERS

ARCHIE'S VICTROLA stands by his back door.
He opens the lid, attaches the trumpet
like a pale morning glory,
winds the springs up tight.

He likes the old songs: The Cowboy Waltz,
Red River Valley, a piano piece called
Balkan Fantasy, although he says
he don't know much about piano music.

"But the fella sure plays fast."
He folds his hands, settles back
in a kitchen chair, nodding time.
"My Ma liked this piece, too."

Sometimes when she was alone, she sang,
or danced doing the housework.
Her photograph hangs over the couch.
It shows her upright, lean,

shaped by desert light into a woman
who didn't smile easily, who folded her arms
across her breasts, shielding softness,
who stood firm in the dust
and stilled her dancing skirts.

OLD PETE

FiRST LIGHT. The old mule
leans against your door
and heaves and coughs,
nose in the dust.

You know what you have to do,
except you never thought
he would follow so easy,
come behind you through new grass
like a hound.

Thirty years is a long time
to be together.
Marriage of a kind.
You touch him—
shoulder and gaunt flank—
but you don't say "So long"
lest he hear
and raise his head.

You leave him where he falls
for coyotes that will feast
this night. And you think
walking back across the pasture,
it takes forever to get home.

ORAL HISTORIES

FOLK TALES

THEY SAY IT HASN'T changed much in a hundred years.
Turkey Creek runs low and still, and damsel flies
bind lovegrass with blue thread.
For John Ringo it was as good a place to die as any,
though quiet for an outlaw. It was a while
before they found him, propped up in a tree
with a hole where his ear had been
and his horse grazing nearby.

Some old men say he was shot on the flat and carried here,
and some say no, the duel was in this field where the grass
leans to the South and the creek widens, settles down
between smooth banks.

There are always old men to say how,
to weave spells as surely as damsel flies.
Old men awake but dreaming still,
who speak the past with gnarled voices.
They believe what they say, having said it often.
John Ringo rises up and rides before them,
and the great white wolf runs down to Mexico.

And I believe, too, because I have sat at their feet
and seen Apaches, buffalo, the Mormon Trail, the Bridger,
and the Santa Fe; the tracks of wagon wheels so deep
they marked the prairie, shaped my sense of shadowed things
like pain and death, the hope in aged voices conjuring.

SANDHILL CRANES
(Santo Domingo Pueblo)

WE SIT ON THE orange-striped couch,
the old woman in a purple dress,
her face a land of gullies, seams, erosions.

It's not the bowl I bargain for that's important.
What I need is the comfort of women talking,
the sound of words that matter.
What I want is forgiveness
for coming with dollars
to buy the spirit of her grandmother
walled in clay.

I tell her I have seen blackbirds
nesting in the cottonwoods,
heard the call of frogs
from the ruins by the river.
And she tells me the cranes flew over
crying long in the moonlight.

Now we are at ease with one another,
wrapped in the music of migrating birds,
in the spirit of the grandmother
who in her bowl left one line broken—
an open door she passes through.

PRESSED FLOWERS
(Turkey Creek, 1982)

FROM THE COUCH you watch, keen-eyed,
though your body, grown old, betrays you.
You fuss at me because nothing is
the way it was,
because your red and white kettle
gives me trouble.
I need two hands to heft it
from the stove and pour,
rinsing suds, dried egg,
a frieze upon cracked plates.

While I struggle,
muscles taut across my back,
I wonder if your women were stronger.
If your mother, who bore ten children,
who planted, laundered, civilized a mountain,
found work easy.

When I have stacked the plates
and wiped the sink
I will ask to see your photographs
of horses, hounds, outlaws with cold eyes.
Scattered among them will be pictures
of women—sweeping, hanging clothes,
feeding a swirl of hens.
Women caught in their chores
like netted butterflies
or flowers cut and dried
between hard covers.

There will be pictures of you
on horseback. No houses could keep you then,
and no woman. It was the mountains you loved.
You understood their desire.

Old man, everything has changed
and nothing.
There will always be men
who ride mountains, dreaming themselves
in the distance. There will always be
women looking after, caught in a flurry of wings.

FLOWERING ALMOND
(For Edith)

YOU FEED THE turtles cat food
   at four o'clock each afternoon,
   let skunks nest behind old doors
   on your porch; the bright-eyed babies
tumble at your feet each night
flashing black fur and wilderness.

Today you take me into your garden
of staked plants, oxalis burning at the gate,
and into your square plains house
with helter-skelter rooms, tables buried
under photographs and doilies, letters,
plants, nuts and colored stones, a bible
and a spool with scarlet thread meandering.

You offer me a pear,
green-gold in a curving dish,
so ripe the juice spills down my chin
like honey-water, and I lick it,
sweeping the last goodness with my tongue
while I read your diaries,
sixty years of valley history recalled...

The white leghorns laid today. First time.
The eggs were fine.
Went up the creek, cut wood, drove the wagon down.
Bought 18 dozen clothespins at the store.
The baby died. Ground so hard we dug all day.
The paint mare foaled a brown stud colt.
My almond tree put out a flower.
Two dry years and cattle dropping.
I lug water to the tree and pray...

What lies in my lap is the coming and going
of lives and seasons; a ritual,
as the twilight whirling of wild babies,
as the branch of your almond tree
laid lightly down along the split rail fence
each spring for years.

Poor Will's Widow

ROAD-FACED AS a cow, with bony knees
and elbows jutting out like fence posts,
you sit, unlikely sinner, in the Sears chair
with the purple throw, sorting peaches while we talk.

I remind myself you are an adulteress,
a fallen woman who moved right in
on Charley and his twenty cats
and loved them all for years.

I ask, wasn't it lonely
back in those mountains,
shunned by the righteous,
by all the wives on market day?

Wasn't it more penance than paradise,
with neither of you young,
fighting the dry years, those cats so wild
they weighed the table down, mealtimes?

You shift, a sack of angles,
neither lush nor schooled in love.
Lonely? No. No time for that,
though Charley never talked a lot.

Those hills were full of talk—
turkeys gobbling, coyotes hunting
down the wash,
and Lord knows, jays are never still.

And all night in summer
the poor-wills calling just like folks.
Poor-will...poor-will...
In bed you'd hear them
a lullaby strung out till dawn.

Poor-will...poor-will...
Two notes. Enough for birds
to make a life.
Enough for a smart woman
who, when a man cares,
don't need a heap of words
to prove it.

THE WEAVERS OF CHIMAYO

TRUCHAS, Trampas, Chimayo...
all the apple trees alight
along high valleys...
Chimayo, where old men with curious eyes
take my hand and call me "Lady."

"Lady. This rug is the finest weave.
From Spain comes the pattern.
From Spain with our grandfathers.
Three hundred years.
Three hundred years ago..."

Yesterday.
A design captured with thread.
Old men who touch
with thin fingers my hand.
"Lady."

And we call them, "Greasers,"
"Wetbacks," "Chicanos."
Everything but what they are:
conquistadores, padres, first colonials,
men and women the same as we
who, from these mountains
from the bones of deserts
from cañons
haciendas
tar paper shacks
pickups
missions
shrines
the worn red bowls
of village plazas

look out across a land that we
turn into missile sites and dusty waste,
home of the chili dog
and the fast-food enchilada,

look out unhumbled,
speak to me,
name me
"Lady."

NEWLYWEDS

THEY SAY WHEN Archie was married
he brought his bride to this rough hill
and pitched a tent. He gave her dishes,
pots and pans to use on the open fire,
a pedal sewing machine. Then he went off,
riding fence.

And she, who from her canvas door
could see a hundred miles or more
across the flat to mountains—
the hump-backed Mules, the Dragoons
piled up like gold—she nagged for a house

with real doors, a porch to rock on
when the wind came up, evenings,
a cook stove like Edith's.
Swept floors, beds with coverlets,
clean windows showed a woman's status,
and she had a right to that.

As for the land, red rocks and sweet-blooming
mesquite, bony hills softened by juniper,
those were a man's things, and good riddance.
Outside, a woman felt exposed, indecent somehow,
with nothing to sweep but a mountain
and no need to polish the sky.

DIFFERENT SEASONS

Y OU RECOLLECT HOW, when you were a boy,
the first hard snow came in November.
By then the barn was filled, the calabazas
stored to feed the pigs through winter.

Come Christmas, the tanks froze so hard
you could drive a team across. Snow
drifted twenty feet deep in the canyons.
Once you fell through it, clean to the bottom,
tunneled out and were blinded by winter light.

I am blinded by what is familiar,
by what I know, or reaching out, can touch.
When you say that long ago, in Spring,
these hawk-scoured fields stretched
green and blooming, I struggle to see
what you see so clearly...

The dust of a thousand cattle on the trail.
The summer cornfields where you hoed
and sometimes slept among the tassels,
dampening the red earth with your sweat.

WOLF

YOU BEGIN now to talk
as if paying for your supper
like a traveling bard, a tale-spinner.
The lamplight is soft on our faces,
on your hands, rope-callused,
hamburgered by machinery.
The little owl is in the oak
accompanying you,
and coyotes sing in the wash.

Once, you say, not too many years ago,
there was a great albino wolf,
the last of all wolves in these hills.
He ran alone, as quick on his silver paws
as dry lightning, and always in moonlight
the color of his eyes.

You'd see him passing down the valley
on his way to Mexico,
and then you'd see him coming back
on the dusty road at midnight
set on his own wolf business.

Once your sheep dog went for him
and they fought, long-shadowed under the moon.
You watched, halfway rooting for the wolf
because he had the mountains in him,
defied a world with his white-throated howl.

He did for the sheep dog.
Got him across the loins and shook him,
threw him up against the fence
like a torn saddle blanket
and bolted, making no sound.

You buried the dog, and mourned a bit,
and went on living.
Trained a redbone hound to run your cattle
and kept an eye on the fields at night
for the wolf running restless from his destiny,
for the last unbroken thing you ever knew.

TRUE STORY

THE ROAD TO JEFFORD's has become a wash.
It's marked by coyote tracks,
criss-crossed by feet of quail,
the hoof prints of two spotted mares
who watch me from the hill and nickering
descend to circle, sniff, and flick
their tails at me.

At the gate the sign says, "Not responsible
for accident or injury while on this property,"
and the road winds into gullies where bull snakes
lie and tarweed coats my boots with resin.

"Jeff," I say, "That road needs fixing."
He tips his hat and looks at me,
thumbing through his hermit's words with care
because I'm female and a man's plain speech
offends some ladies.

He sets his jaw, and halfway meets my eye, and shuffles
like a boy, shy, overwhelmed by femininity, and says,
"I had that road done right and graded, too,
then Ken come along and did it his way. Did it wrong.
Dumb asshole bugger."

NEIGHBORS

CHICKEN JO LIVES up French Canyon
in a tin-roofed shack
with no plumbing.

She sells chickens to the fort,
eggs, too. For herself
she prefers the neighbors' beef,

steals a calf every payday
when the boys show up
to eat, drink, take her
to the backroom where
she drums her heels into the springs
as if she were sixteen again,

small, white, sleek
as feathers
in unrestrained moonlight.

COWBOYS AND INDIANS
(Turkey Creek, Arizona, 1981)

YOU ARE TELLING how your dad rode
the U.S. Mail, and every now and then
was chased by Apaches who roasted mescal
in a pit up near Sanders' fence.
When they'd get to feeling good
they'd come out hollering
and give your dad a run for it.
No reason. Just remembering the days
before peace turned time slow.

Your dad homesteaded and set up
a blacksmith's forge. He fixed
what needed fixing without questions.
A man's business was his own, he figured.

You were a boy then, fascinated by the forge,
the fire, the way your dad could lift hot metal
in his hands and not get burned. And you
and an old Apache would sit in the shadows
and watch all day and sway with the hammering
and never talk, though sometimes you'd give
the Indian a piece of jerky and he'd take it,
nod, and go to chewing, watching the sparks rise,
the iron smoking as it cooled.

You remember the day Luther Price and Clyde Rivers
come in, got to boasting. Clyde, the dandy,
small and swaggering, who always wore a pair
of studded leather gauntlets, or carried them
and slapped his palm for emphasis.
You remember that, the sound of gloves tapping,
and Clyde saying your father's dried-up well
was a damn good place to hide a crime.

And you remember how your father,
who minded no man's business but his own,
rode out with the vigilantes that same night
and pulled Tar Wilson's body feet first
from the well.

Luther took the rap, got hanged,
but Clyde, well, he just disappeared.
Was here that day and gone the next,
and you always figured the old Apache got him...

But that Indian and Clyde's another story.
The moon's already clear past Chiricahua Peak,
and first light comes right early
in the summer.

THE JESUS WAGON

LEBAN KLINGHOFER got religion
and gave up farming
to drive the Jesus wagon.

He took his white pickup
built a lean-to on the back
painted it with crooked red letters.

Jesus is coming, it says,
and the plagues of Egypt.
Have you cleansed your soul?

He drives slowly down
the backroads
searching out sinners.

Now he's parked at my gate.
His hump-backed truck
blots out the mountains;

its wheel hubs spit weeds
like tobacco.
Leban's come to save my soul.

I'd like to blast him straight to Jesus.
I'd like to grab his neck
and squeeze and say,

"Leban, the 'J' on Jesus is backwards,
and you've parked between me
and God."

PICKUP

UNDER MY HANDS your old truck
bucks the stones
and leaps the wash, a wild thing,
though I hold it to a crawl
feeling you sprawled
on the metal bed behind.

You have trusted me to drive,
to take you to town and back,
two hundred miles of rattle
with cattle on their watch
along the ditch where spotted snakes
stretch sleeping in the sun.

And you urge me on,
your old eyes impudent and blue
putting pain aside to split the valleys,
scatter tumbleweed, move South with me
as if you were a young man quick with dreams.

Your sleep leaves me in command,
seated high, a dry wind rampant
in my hair, the space of desert
running wide at either hand...

a timeless but imperfect wilderness
like love.

Two Women at the Little Bighorn

HERE WHERE THE prairie curves in upon itself
like the thighs of a woman asleep,
and the sage spreads, rooted in bone,
a Crow woman leads me to the Battlefield.

Her voice falls into coulees, rises
to ghostly ridges. Her hands describe
a rain of arrows, fallen horses,
swift knives severing fingers, heads.

We walk softly. There are too many hearts
under the grasses. Too great a price
paid for this hour.

Her name, she tells me,
is Burn Cedar as Incense,
and her syllables spill out like water,
touch the air like the wings
of the black, beaked bird.*

I have nothing so beautiful to offer.
No words for victory or plunder, and
few apologies. Across the rift of war
we face each other, separate
despite the pain of gender.

It is not her people buried here
but mine.

Absaroka, the mythical black bird from which the white man derived the name "Crow."

REQUIEM FOR A COWBOY
(For Archie Smith, 1912-1983)

WHEN I GO down the road
past the hill the red bull guards,
when I go down through sunflowers,
through all the weeds whose names
and reasons I absorbed from you
and loved like rain,

when I go down to your locked blue house,
empty and stripped of shadows,
your bright mare comes, tossing her head,
and the grey burro,
sighing splinters like a saw.
They dance on gentle hooves
look past me for you out of habit,
loneliness, love.

Each evening we meet at the gate,
eager as dogs or children.
The mare nuzzles my shoulder.
The burro pushes gnarled flanks
against my thighs. Sometimes
I turn around, hoping to see you
on your way somewhere
or coming toward us carrying grain.

And sometimes the old burro
lifts long ears and leans
toward the rutted road
as if she can hear you
taking the hill,
hurrying home before dark.

NIGHT SONGS

I have been walking the colicky horse
for six hours; round and round, me singing—
Red River Valley, The Streets of Laredo—
the old songs in four/four time.

His muzzle droops on my shoulder,
his warm breath spills down my neck,
and every now and then he moans in my ear
and plants his feet firmly in the dust.

He can't lie down; can't roll.
That's the point of this promenade.
A twisted gut and he dies, screaming,
a thousand pounds of agony.

So we walk—and talk and sing—
and he keeps coming, thoroughbred
to the bone, giving his heart
to the sound of my voice,

while around us in the dark
the mating cry of the nighthawk rises,
spills like water, floods the fields
and lifts us into a dream that could go on
till morning.

THIS VALLEY
THIS SKY

TRANSFORMATIONS
(Cochiti Pueblo)

YOU COME DOWN out of the mountains
and leave the snow behind.
At Cochiti the earth appears again,
red, gold, shaped like the living.

You remember that the Indians were dancing
here last summer. The beat of the drums
stole upward into your heart.
You swayed with it, stamped, snorted,

knew the deer, the coyote, and the buffalo.
Next to you sat an old woman wrapped in a rainbow
and swaying to the same time. After awhile
you looked at her and knew yourself.

II

You wonder whether these plains ache
in winter or whether you ache for them,
your bones moaning under your skin.
You wonder where the boundary is
that divides you from ground
and if it has a name.

Bodies make no sound when loins melt down
and only wind is breathing.
If you were to lie down silent
among the grama, the sage,
and stay a long time,
there would be no difference
between you.

WILD GINGER

TO SEE THIS FLOWER, you must lie down
in old leaves, moss, the peaty rubble
of years, tilt the brown bell upward,
and with your eyes descend
through darkness into light.

This is the hard part.
You must leave your body
sprawling in the dirt,
and like a bee approach the heart.

What you know is useless here.
You have no language
for your sinking spiral
intent upon its mark,

that octagonal chamber
where amber stamens rise and wait.
They appease a different hunger.
That which wakes you from
the dark sleep after love
crying
Touch me.

CALLA LILIES
(For Georgia O'Keeffe)

WE SHOULD ALL see things so simply...
the basics of bone
the sky unchanging blue
sandhills that endure
despite eroding thighs.

We should remember
these curving shapes
are what we are,
and move with similar precision
toward the light.

Leaves reaching through darkness
crack pale stones,
persist,
bear scented strength in secret
until blooming time.

Perhaps we should strive
for their courage
in those acts that need no guidance—
the flamboyant thrust of stamens
up and out of opening petals.

LETTER FROM SAN PEDRO
(For Leah)

YOU WRITE THAT the leaves
    are falling,
that you stand at your window
    and watch them
scarlet and orange,
caught by the wind.

Here there are no leaves,
    only grass to the edges of sky,
and it is lovely as animals,
    silver, dun, old gold.

When I open my door,
whole fields arch their backs,
run under my feet
without bit or bridle,
    knowing no master
      at all.

ENDANGERED SPECIES
(Animas, New Mexico)

THE SIGHT of antelope
always startles.
I think the land is moving,
then something in me jumps
and follows, hoofed, horned,
facing the wind.

Once there were so many
the prairie stayed in motion
like the sea.
I know this,
and I know that life
hangs by a thread,

that running does not answer
or even staying still
crouched in rock shadow
behind black brush strokes of sage.

THE ARRESTED DANCE

BEND. STRETCH. ARMS raised, lifting the sheet to the line,
I see myself, a dancer, carved with repeating rhythm on
a frieze.
There are women by streams beating clothes,
working at the edges of fields. They lift their arms against the sky,
stop where the line holds taut.

Bend. Stretch. My mother, humming,
hangs her wash in the shade of morning glories.
Her reach is confined to blue bowl.
She does not look out, or looking,
does not see beyond her hands.

Bend. Stretch. I have succumbed to motion, become the dance.
Though today the singing of locusts, the scream of a hawk
make variation on an ancient theme,
it is the gesture—rage or supplication—
that endures.

MOONRISE, HERNANDEZ
(For Ansel Adams)

IT IS NOT yet night,
but we stand waiting
for the moon to come,
for the first thin slice
to deepen dark places.

Its quick leap,
its sudden light
do nothing to dispel
our solitude.
There are needs in us
for which we have only silence.

If someone would photograph
this moonrise
we would show in the foreground,
head stones, sorrowing,
side by side.

NINE SMOOTH HILLS

DRIVING I COME upon them—
three rows of three hills
that ripple across the valley
like the bodies of women
asleep a thousand years.

Grass has covered them
and their toes have blended
with the earth. In their huge
loins, cows give birth,
arching their backs against stone.

I think they will never awaken,
these mounded Amazons enamored
of ease, these mothers enchanted
with nurturing, these ladies
dreaming wind and the sweep
of seasons while digging themselves
always more deeply into the ground.

UNENDING
(Ingomar, Montana)

YOU FEEL THE grasses bending
in your bones. Wheat grass,
brome, blue-stem bleached bronze
by summer.

If you put out your hands
whole prairies would ripple there,
dance in your palms
curve like haunches
drop off into the wide air.

It is always a question
of how far you can see
how wide you can open
how willing to fill
and empty again
how much you are able to hold.

NEARING MAGDALENA

WE ARE MOVING THROUGH the open spaces now,
great, gaunt plains scarred by raven's wings,
mountains, naked as hearts.
We are no one here,
       nowhere,
yet we touch carefully
knowing freedom is deceptive as sunlight.

Like shadows we lean toward one another
then away, learning our hungers,
keeping them still
until touch is bearable.
Until you can put out your hand
and I can fold round you
like a glove.

FORECAST
(The Border Country, Arizona, 1987)

THE GRASS IS browning over, we say,
with the satisfaction of pasture watchers.
And we say it until it happens,
the way we forecast rain
    and birthings.

Doomed by distance,
we draw seasons around us
for vindication.
Mountain-seared,
tattooed by clouds,
marked as surely as the storms
mark courses in the sand,

we wait for change,
tied by our eyes
to this valley
this sky.

THE RAINMAKER

I WAS INTRODUCED to a rancher
in the lobby of the Copper Queen Hotel.
He took off his hat (they all do that,
making me want to curtsey)
and he said, "We measured two inches
up Turkey Creek yesterday."

Rain. Clouds. Water.
Their lack erases thought,
forms all conversation.
On high mesas Indians dance
draw lightning in blowing sand.
Here, the last rainmaker
with pinwheels, smoke sticks, bells,
stands singing on a stone,
and conjures clouds.

I think I could walk in there naked
and no one would notice.
But if I said, "Rain."
If I said, "The tank rose ten feet
overnight, and the wash is running
like a highway," then all eyes
would find me. Then they'd say,
"Hey! It's been five years
since Cottonwood overflowed.
You want to try our place next?"

POTPOURRI

I HAVE whole days
mixed in the Indian basket.
Lavender, moss roses,
wild sage, the dry high country
singing in a branch,
darting between thought,
slantings of light,
moments of falling
and rising again.

To bury my face in the basket
is to walk barefoot
on all the diverse earths
with eight winds blowing at once.

SEPTEMBER: THE VALLEY
(The Border Country, 1987)

IT HAPPENS so quickly.
You uncoil like the tongue
of hummingbird
or moth,

leave your body
become the purple air,
and who you were
does not matter,
or where.

Only the reaching
is important.
Only the loveliness of miles.

EINE KLEINE NACHTMUSIK

I HARDLY SLEPT that summer.
The mockingbird and I
kept company, and he
sang symphonies, a fountain
bursting from the midst of leaves.

We watched the nights together,
applauded moonrise. In silence
I touched with my eyes,
reached out and lifted shadows

while the trees recreated themselves
and whole mountains took root;
while the plain stretched south,
silver-haired, never-ending,

while music poured
from that small, winged flute—
so joyful
   so fearless
      so confident of time.

BLUE MORNING RISING

KILLDEER HAUNT the ponds
in the blue morning
and larks surge, singing,
from sleep.

I move slowly
away from you,
your gentle breath,
the solemnity of your dreaming.

No lark, no sparrow even,
I will myself into wing flutter
into a whisper
into a rising
like light.

LEAVING THE VALLEY

THE STUBBORN die alone
in these vast valleys
in mountains empty
of all but the tenacious few
who, shaped by rock and sky,
prefer to die in solitude.

They're found then,
stiffened in sleep,
frozen over uneaten dinners,
curled up in pastures swept
by wings of hawks.
And always the living
clutch themselves and cry
of doctors, nursing homes,
accoutrements that should have been.

But dying is a lonely thing—
a parting of selves—
and those who choose the simple way
know best. They go forth
armed with remembrances—
red earth, yellow grass,
and startling passing over of days.

ABOUT THE AUTHOR

JANE CANDIA COLEMAN has had a life-long love affair with the West. Born in Pittsburgh, Pennsylvania, she earned a degree in creative writing from the University of Pittsburgh and later co-founded and directed the Women's Creative Writing Center at Carlow College in Pittsburgh.

She now owns a horse ranch where she resides near Rodeo, New Mexico, and writes full-time. Her prize-winning book of fiction, *The Voices of Doves*, was published in 1988. A second fiction collection, *Stories from Mesa Country*, is forthcoming from Ohio State University Press/Swallow Press, and a chapbook of satirical poetry, *Deep in his Heart JR Is Laughing at Us*, is forthcoming from Adastra Press.